THE OPTIONS STRATEGY SECRETS

Contents

Introduction

Options Trading Strategies for Beginners

5 Options Trading Strategies For Beginners

Finding the Right Option Strategy

Which Is The Most Successful Options Strategy?

Safe Option Strategies To Boost Your Trading Profits

Conclusion

Introduction

Options strategies are great tools for diversification of your options trading portfolio. Diversification means that a traders includes a variety of options buying and options selling strategies as tools for protecting and growing his portfolio. As a beginner cruising through a long list of options strategies, you may find it difficult and overwhelming to navigate all of the options. Schaeffer's Investment Research, the best options newsletter publishers in the world, can help you.

Choosing from strategies suitable for bullish markets, bearish markets, high volatility, sideways, and unknown environments and then following the strategy for optimization can prove to be quite a task. It is especially important to make an informed decision about which options strategies to include in your trading portfolio.

Options Trading Strategies for Beginners

Every trader has at least one goal in common; to make money. And learning about different options trading strategies will provide you with the information you need to accomplish this goal. Therefore, take the time to review the top seven options trading strategies listed below. In fact, the way you create daily wealth may change forever. There are many strategies available to traders. But let's learn the basics first and pretty soon you'll be ready to tackle the more complex strategies. So, let's get started…
Writing down the best options trading strategies
Understanding Options Trading Strategies

1. Long Call – Capture Outsized Gains from Higher Stock Prices

This is one of the preferred strategies for traders who are bullish. This means you are betting the stock price will rise and do so by buying calls. Call options are contracts that give their holder the right – but not the obligation – to buy shares at a certain price. It's essentially a bet that the price of the underlying stock will rise above the option's strike price and the contracts will give their owner the ability to buy at a discount. When that happens, those calls are referred to as "in the money." If a call option's strike price is above the price of its underlying security, it's referred to as "out of the money."
Let's use stock "X" as an example. A trader is betting that X shares will exceed $250 per share by the third Friday in July. The higher the share price goes over the strike price, the more money the trader will make.
For this hypothetical example, let's say that stock X trades for around $248, just under your $250 strike price. The July 15th $250 options trade for around $4.35. This means that X's stock would have to be at $254.35 for the trader to break even. So, say you lock out and news of a new product drops the day after the trader bought their calls. This news caused X's share price to climb to $256.35. That means the trader exceeded their breakeven point by $2 and their options are now worth $6.35. This is good for a gain of 45% (you entered the calls for $4.35 and they moved up to $6.35). This is an example using intrinsic value to show you how you can profit from going long on a call option. In many cases, a big move up in the stock can hand you even bigger moves on the options. You may experience bigger returns as a result.

2. Long Put: How to Profit from Downward Stock Movements – With Less Risk Than Short selling

This is one of the preferred options trading strategies for traders who are bearish. This means the trader is betting the stock price will fall. A put works the opposite way of a call. If a put options strike price is above the stock's market price, it's in the money. If the strike price is below the stock's market price, it's out of the money. And if a trader buys a put option, they are expecting the stock price to fall below the strike price by expiration. Puts give the holder the right – but, again, not the obligation – to sell shares of a stock at a certain price.

Let's use stock "X" as an example again. And the trader takes stock X's current $248 price and buys puts that expire on July 15th with a strike price of $247.50, for a premium (cost) of $5.20. For these puts, their breakeven point would be $242.30. Just like with the calls, but in reverse. If stock X moves below that breakeven point, the trader will profit. Say news of a scandal breaks, and stock X's share price drops to $238 over the course of a few days. The traders put would climb to $9.50. As a result, they could sell them for a gain of 82.7% and a $4.30 profit.

3. Covered Call: Unlock Additional Income from Your Stocks

Choosing what options trading strategies work best for you can be challenging if you're not versed in all the different types. So let's continue with a two-part strategy known as a covered call. This strategy requires the lowest level of permission from your broker and can be done in any type of account. It also requires the trader to own shares of the underlying stock (100 shares for every option contract). It is important to note that the trader is selling to open the calls against their position. They will buy a stock, at least 100 shares and sell an option against their holdings. When a trader does this, they are reducing their cost by the option premium received. In exchange for that reduction, they also limit their upside to the strike price of the option sold.

For example, if you buy stock "Y" for $10 and you sell an option with a $12 strike for $1, your cost is now $9. However, your upside is limited to the spread between $9 and $12. If the shares expire below the option strike price, you keep the stock and the option premium. If the shares are above the price at or before expiration, the shares can be called or taken out of your account as long as you are paid the strike price. Writing a covered call involves selling an option against a stock you already own. This generates income while you are holding it. It's a great strategy for income seekers.

4. Bull Call Spread: Going Long for A Lower Cost

A bull call spread is the simplest type of spread. It's often referred to as a vertical call spread. For this strategy, you would buy a lower strike call and sell a higher strike call. It is very similar to doing a covered call trade with a stock where you buy the stock and sell an option against it.

The goal is to reduce your cost by selling an option against the option that you bought. The options can be really expensive and this is a way to reduce your cost. The bull call spread or vertical call spread is when you are betting on the price of the shares moving higher. When you are betting the shares will move lower, you would use a bear put spread. This is otherwise known as a vertical put spread, which I explain in more detail below.

5. Bear Put Spread: Lowering Your Hedge Costs

A bear put spread is the same concept as a bull call spread. But instead of using calls, you are using puts. You buy a put at the higher strike price and sell another put, with the same expiration date, at a lower price.
Let's say you buy a $10 put for $2 and sell a $5 put for $1. Your cost would be $1 and your spread would be $5. You are betting the shares will go to $5 or lower to collect the whole spread. But, any move below $9 will result in a profit. If the stock was at $20 and you expected it to drop to $15, you would buy to open the $20 strike option and sell to open the $15 strike option. If the $20 put was at $3 and the $15 put was at $1.50, your cost would be $1.50 and your spread would be $5.
 This strategy is not a pure short position. It's a hedge, meaning that you have to have long positions which you are trying to protect. Since this strategy is a spread, your losses will be limited as both the long and short sides of the trade will go lower. One should only use this strategy if they understand how a hedge trade works.

6. Long Strangle: Win Not Matter Which Way A Stock Moves

A strangle is one of the most popular strategies and best applied in situations where the underlying shares are volatile and prone to rapid moves in either direction. It's sister strategy is called a straddle, which I'll explain in a bit. This strategy allows you to profit no matter which way the stock moves, as long as a stock moves a certain amount in either direction. A trader will buy an out-of-the-money call option and a put option at the same time with the same expiration date. Yet, they will have different strike prices. The put strike price should be below the call strike price.
 Let's say you're looking at shares in company "A". It's currently trading at $15. But it's incredibly volatile and an earnings announcement is coming that could really move the stock. As such, you think it could rapidly drop to $5 or shoot up to $25. You'd be looking to buy puts with a strike price below $15 and calls with a strike price above $15.

You find two perfect ones, puts with a strike price of $10 and calls with a strike price of $20. You will need company A to drop to $8 or rise to $22 to break even. However, any move above $22 or below $8 will net you the profit you're looking for. So, say the shares move down to $5 like you predicted. You would make $5 minus the $2 you paid for the put and the call. That'd be a net return of $3, or 150% on the entire trade. The same would be true if the share price shot up to $25. Strangles are best played around earnings season, which is when companies report earnings. And those reports can lead to big swings in stock prices. Now let's get into the last of the top seven options trading strategies every investor should know.

7. Long Straddle: Up or Down Movement... You Win

Straddles and strangles are two strategies that allow a trader to benefit whether a stock moves up or down. So, let's discuss what the key difference is between these two strategies. A straddle is very similar to a strangle, in that an investor will buy a call option and a put option at the same time. But both options should have the same strike price AND expiration date.

In a straddle, typically you will get something back (unless they pin it at your strike exactly). Strangles and straddles are pretty much up to the investor to decide what fits their personal style and trading needs.

The Bottom Line

The main advantage of options is that they give you leverage on the markets to help you maximize your gains. There are a variety of options trading strategies for investors to profit from. And today, you've learned some of the most popular ones. Take time to learn the process and pretty soon your goal to make money will come.

Now that you know the basics, you're ready to continue your trading journey. There's no better way to do so than by signing up to receive Trade of the Day. It's a FREE e-letter providing information on the latest and greatest stock plays, investment opportunities, option trading strategies and more… Subscribe below to receive this premium content straight to your inbox!

5 Options Trading Strategies For Beginners

1. Long call

In this strategy, the trader buys a call – referred to as "going long" a call – and expects the stock price to exceed the strike price by expiration. The upside on this trade is uncapped, if the stock soars, and traders can earn many times their initial investment.
Example: Stock X is trading for $20 per share, and a call with a strike price of $20 and expiration in four months is trading at $1. The contract costs $100, or one contract * $1 * 100 shares represented per contract.

Here's the profit on the long call at expiration:

Reward/risk: In this example, the trader breaks even at $21 per share, or the strike price plus the $1 premium paid. Above $20, the option increases in value by $100 for every dollar the stock increases. The option expires worthless when the stock is at the strike price and below.
The upside on a long call is theoretically unlimited. If the stock continues to rise before expiration, the call can keep climbing higher, too. For this reason long calls are one of the most popular ways to wager on a rising stock price.
The downside on a long call is a total loss of your investment, $100 in this example. If the stock finishes below the strike price, the call will expire worthless and you'll be left with nothing.
When to use it: A long call is a good choice when you expect the stock to rise significantly before the option's expiration. If the stock rises only a little above the strike price, the option may still be in the money, but may not even return the premium paid, leaving you with a net loss.

2. Covered call

A covered call involves selling a call option ("going short") but with a twist. Here the trader sells a call but also buys the stock underlying the option, 100 shares for each call sold. Owning the stock turns a potentially risky trade – the short call – into a relatively safe trade that can generate income. Traders expect the stock price to be below the strike price at expiration. If the stock finishes above the strike price, the owner must sell the stock to the call buyer at the strike price.

Example: Stock X is trading for $20 per share, and a call with a strike price of $20 and expiration in four months is trading at $1. The contract pays a premium of $100, or one contract * $1 * 100 shares represented per contract. The trader buys 100 shares of stock for $2,000 and sells one call to receive $100.

Here's the profit on the covered call strategy:

Reward/risk: In this example, the trader breaks even at $19 per share, or the strike price minus the $1 premium received. Below $19, the trader would lose money, as the stock would lose money, more than offsetting the $1 premium. At exactly $20, the trader would keep the full premium and hang onto the stock, too. Above $20, the gain is capped at $100. While the short call loses $100 for every dollar increase above $20, it's totally offset by the stock's gain, leaving the trader with the initial $100 premium received as the total profit.

The upside on the covered call is limited to the premium received, regardless of how high the stock price rises. You can't make any more than that, but you can lose a lot more. Any gain that you otherwise would have made with the stock rise is completely offset by the short call.

The downside is a complete loss of the stock investment, assuming the stock goes to zero, offset by the premium received. The covered call leaves you open to a significant loss, if the stock falls. For instance, in our example if the stock fell to zero the total loss would be $1,900.

When to use it: A covered call can be a good strategy to generate income if you already own the stock and don't expect the stock to rise significantly in the near future. So the strategy can transform your already-existing holdings into a source of cash. The covered call is popular with older investors who need the income, and it can be useful in tax-advantaged accounts where you might otherwise pay taxes on the premium and capital gains if the stock is called.

3. Long put

In this strategy, the trader buys a put – referred to as "going long" a put – and expects the stock price to be below the strike price by expiration. The upside on this trade can be many multiples of the initial investment, if the stock falls significantly. Example: Stock X is trading for $20 per share, and a put with a strike price of $20 and expiration in four months is trading at $1. The contract costs $100, or one contract * $1 * 100 shares represented per contract.

Here's the profit on the long put at expiration:

Reward/risk: In this example, the put breaks even when the stock closes at option expiration at $19 per share, or the strike price minus the $1 premium paid. Below $19 the put increases in value $100 for every dollar decline in the stock. Above $20, the put expires worthless and the trader loses the full premium of $100.

The upside on a long put is almost as good as on a long call, because the gain can be multiples of the option premium paid. However, a stock can never go below zero, capping the upside, whereas the long call has theoretically unlimited upside. Long puts are another simple and popular way to wager on the decline of a stock, and they can be safer than shorting a stock.

The downside on a long put is capped at the premium paid, $100 here. If the stock closes above the strike price at expiration of the option, the put expires worthless and you'll lose your investment.

When to use it: A long put is a good choice when you expect the stock to fall significantly before the option expires. If the stock falls only slightly below the strike price, the option will be in the money, but may not return the premium paid, handing you a net loss.

4. Short put

This strategy is the flipside of the long put, but here the trader sells a put – referred to as "going short" a put – and expects the stock price to be above the strike price by expiration. In exchange for selling a put, the trader receives a cash premium, which is the most a short put can earn. If the stock closes below the strike price at option expiration, the trader must buy it at the strike price.

Example: Stock X is trading for $20 per share, and a put with a strike price of $20 and expiration in four months is trading at $1. The contract pays a premium of $100, or one contract * $1 * 100 shares represented per contract.

Here's the profit on the short put at expiration:

Reward/risk: In this example, the short put breaks even at $19, or the strike price less the premium received. Below $19, the short put costs the trader $100 for every dollar decline in price, while above $20 the put seller earns the full $100 premium. Between $19 and $20, the put seller would earn some but not all of the premium.

The upside on the short put is never more than the premium received, $100 here. Like the short call or covered call, the maximum return on a short put is what the seller receives upfront.

The downside of a short put is the total value of the underlying stock minus the premium received, and that would happen if the stock went to zero. In this example, the trader would have to buy $2,000 of the stock (100 shares * $20 strike price), but this would be offset by the $100 premium received, for a total loss of $1,900. When to use it: A short put is an appropriate strategy when you expect the stock to close at the strike price or above at expiration of the option. The stock needs to be only at or above the strike price for the option to expire worthless, letting you keep the whole premium received.

Your broker will want to make sure you have enough equity in your account to buy the stock, if it's put to you. Many traders will hold enough cash in their account to purchase the stock, if the put finishes in the money.

5. Married put

This strategy is like the long put with a twist. The trader owns the underlying stock and also buys a put. This is a hedged trade, in which the trader expects the stock to rise but wants "insurance" in the event that the stock falls. If the stock does fall, the long put offsets the decline.

Example: Stock X is trading for $20 per share, and a put with a strike price of $20 and expiration in four months is trading at $1. The contract costs $100, or one contract * $1 * 100 shares represented per contract. The trader buys 100 shares of stock for $2,000 and buys one put for $100.

Here's the profit on the married put strategy:

Reward/risk: In this example, the married put breaks even at $21, or the strike price plus the cost of the $1 premium. Below $20, the long put offsets the decline in the stock dollar for dollar. Above $21, the total profit increases $100 for every dollar increase in the stock, though the put expires worthless and the trader loses the full amount of the premium paid, $100 here.

The maximum upside of the married put is theoretically uncapped, as long as the stock continues rising, minus the cost of the put. The married put is a hedged position, and so the premium is the cost of insuring the stock and giving it the opportunity to rise with limited downside.

The downside of the married put is the cost of the premium paid. As the value of the stock position falls, the put increases in value, covering the decline dollar for dollar. Because of this hedge, the trader only loses the cost of the option rather than the bigger stock loss.

When to use it: A married put can be a good choice when you expect a stock's price to rise significantly before the option's expiration, but you think it may have a chance to fall significantly, too. The married put allows you to hold the stock and enjoy the potential upside if it rises, but still be covered from substantial loss if the stock falls. For example, a trader might be awaiting news, such as earnings, that may drive the stock up or down, and wants to be covered.

Finding the Right Option Strategy

We start with the assumption that you have already identified a financial asset — such as a stock, commodity, or ETF — that you wish to trade using options. You may have picked this underlying using a stock screener, by employing your own analysis, or by using third-party research. Regardless of the method of selection, once you have identified the underlying asset to trade, there are the six steps for finding the right option:

Formulate your investment objective.

Determine your risk-reward payoff.
Check the volatility.
Identify events.
Devise a strategy.
Establish option parameters.
The six steps follow a logical thought process that makes it easier to pick a specific option for trading. Let's breakdown what each of these steps involves.

1. Option Objective

The starting point when making any investment is your investment objective, and options trading is no different. What objective do you want to achieve with your option trade? Is it to speculate on a bullish or bearish view of the underlying asset? Or is it to hedge potential downside risk on a stock in which you have a significant position?
Are you putting on the trade to earn income from selling option premium? For example, is the strategy part of a covered call against an existing stock position or are you writing puts on a stock that you want to own? Using options to generate income is a vastly different approach compared to buying options to speculate or to hedge. Your first step is to formulate what the objective of the trade is, because it forms the foundation for the subsequent steps.

2. Risk/Reward

The next step is to determine your risk-reward payoff, which should be dependent on your risk tolerance or appetite for risk. If you are a conservative investor or trader, then aggressive strategies such as writing puts or buying a large amount of deep out of the money (OTM) options may not be suited to you. Every option strategy has a well-defined risk and reward profile, so make sure you understand it thoroughly.

3. Check the Volatility

Implied volatility is one of the most important determinants of an option's price, so get a good read on the level of implied volatility for the options you are considering. Compare the level of implied volatility with the stock's historical volatility and the level of volatility in the broad market, since this will be a key factor in identifying your option trade/strategy.

Implied volatility lets you know whether other traders are expecting the stock to move a lot or not. High implied volatility will push up premiums, making writing an option more attractive, assuming the trader thinks volatility will not keep increasing (which could increase the chance of the option being exercised). Low implied volatility means cheaper option premiums, which is good for buying options if a trader expects the underlying stock will move enough to increase the value of the options.

4. Identify Events

Events can be classified into two broad categories: market-wide and stock-specific. Market-wide events are those that impact the broad markets, such as Federal Reserve announcements and economic data releases. Stock-specific events are things like earnings reports, product launches, and spinoffs.

An event can have a significant effect on implied volatility before its actual occurrence, and the event can have a huge impact on the stock price when it does occur. So do you want to capitalize on the surge in volatility before a key event, or would you rather wait on the sidelines until things settle down? Identifying events that may impact the underlying asset can help you decide on the appropriate time frame and expiration date for your option trade.

5. Devise a Strategy

Based on the analysis conducted in the previous steps, you now know your investment objective, desired risk-reward payoff, level of implied and historical volatility, and key events that may affect the underlying asset. Going through the four steps makes it much easier to identify a specific option strategy.

For example, let's say you are a conservative investor with a sizable stock portfolio and want to earn premium income before companies commence reporting their quarterly earnings in a couple of months. You may, therefore, opt for a covered call writing strategy, which involves writing calls on some or all of the stocks in your portfolio.

As another example, if you are an aggressive investor who likes long shots and is convinced that the markets are headed for a big decline within six months, you may decide to buy puts on major stock indices.

6. Establish Parameters

Now that you have identified the specific option strategy you want to implement, all that remains is to establish option parameters like expiration dates, strike prices, and option deltas. For example, you may want to buy a call with the longest possible expiration but at the lowest possible cost, in which case an out-of-the-money call may be suitable. Conversely, if you desire a call with a high delta, you may prefer an in-the-money option.

ITM vs. OTM

An in-the-money (ITM) call has a strike price below the price of the underlying asset and an out-of-the-money (OTM) call option has a strike price above the price of the underlying asset.

Examples Using these Steps

Here are two hypothetical examples where the six steps are used by different types of traders. Say a conservative investor owns 1,000 shares of McDonald's (MCD) and is concerned about the possibility of a 5%+ decline in the stock over the next few months. The investor does not want to sell the stock but does want protection against a possible decline:

Objective: Hedge downside risk in current McDonald's holding (1,000 shares); the stock (MCD) is trading at $161.48.
Risk/Reward: The investor does not mind a little risk as long as it is quantifiable, but is loath to take on unlimited risk.
Volatility: Implied volatility on ITM put options (strike price of $165) is 17.38% for one-month puts and 16.4% for three-month puts. Market volatility, as measured by the CBOE Volatility Index (VIX), is 13.08%.
Events: The investor wants a hedge that extends past McDonald's earnings report. Earnings come out in just over two months, which means the options should extend about three months out.
Strategy: Buy puts to hedge the risk of a decline in the underlying stock.
Option Parameters: Three-month $165-strike-price puts are available for $7.15.
Since the investor wants to hedge the stock position past earnings, they buy the three-month $165 puts. The total cost of the put position to hedge 1,000 shares of MCD is $7,150 ($7.15 x 100 shares per contract x 10 contracts). This cost excludes commissions.
If the stock drops, the investor is hedged, as the gain on the put option will likely offset the loss in the stock. If the stock stays flat and is trading unchanged at $161.48 very shortly before the puts expire, the puts would have an intrinsic value of $3.52 ($165 - $161.48), which means that the investor could recoup about $3,520 of the amount invested in the puts by selling the puts to close the position. If the stock price goes up above $165, the investor profits on the increase in value of the 1,000 shares but forfeits the $7,150 paid on the options

Now, assume an aggressive trader is bullish on the prospects for Bank of America (BAC) and has $1,000 to implement an options trading strategy:

Objective: Buy speculative calls on Bank of America. The stock is trading at $30.55.

Risk/Reward: The investor does not mind losing the entire investment of $1,000, but wants to get as many options as possible to maximize potential profit.

Volatility: Implied volatility on OTM call options (strike price of $32) is 16.9% for one-month calls and 20.04% for four-month calls. Market volatility as measured by the CBOE Volatility Index (VIX) is 13.08%.

Events: None, the company just had earnings so it will be a few months before the next earnings announcement. The investor is not concerned with earnings right now, but believes the stock market will rise over the next few months and believes this stock will do especially well.

Strategy: Buy OTM calls to speculate on a surge in the stock price.

Option Parameters: Four-month $32 calls on BAC are available at $0.84, and four-month $33 calls are offered at $0.52.

Since the investor wants to purchase as many cheap calls as possible, they opt for the four-month $33 calls. Excluding commissions, 19 contracts are bought or $0.52 each, for a cash outlay of $988 (19 x $0.52 x 100 = $988), plus commissions.

The maximum gain is theoretically infinite. If a global banking conglomerate comes along and offers to acquire Bank of America for $40 in the next couple of months, the $33 calls would be worth at least $7 each, and the option position would be worth $13,300. The breakeven point on the trade is the $33 + $0.52, or $33.52.

If the stock is above $33.01 at expiration, it is in-the-money, has value, and will be subject to auto-exercise. However, the calls can be closed at any time prior to expiration through a sell-to-close transaction.

Note that the strike price of $33 is 8% higher than the stock's current price. The investor must be confident that the price can move up by at least 8% in the next four months. If the price isn't above the $33 strike price at expiry, the investor will have lost the $988.

Which Is The Most Successful Options Strategy?

So, if you should avoid buying stocks and selling straddles and strangles, what is the most successful options strategy? The most successful options strategy is to sell out-of-the-money put and call options. This options strategy has a high probability of profit - you can also use credit spreads to reduce risk. If done correctly, this strategy can yield ~40% annual returns. David Jaffee has experienced considerable success selling option premium, and he has taught more than 1,500 students to do the same.
Many options trading courses and coaches encourage traders to be very active, but David Jaffee has found this strategy to be unsuccessful. In his course, David Jaffee teaches students how to be patient when trading options. By making only one or two trades per week, you can still earn impressive profits. Patience is rewarded with successful trades. Selling option premium reduces your risk and carries a higher probability of profit. In fact, selling option premium is significantly less risky than buying and selling stocks or buying options.
Over time, small and consistent profits add up considerably. You will not get rich overnight by selling option premium, but you can compound your profits and earn considerable gains.
Is there a guaranteed profit options strategy?
There are very few guarantees in life.
David Jaffee has found that selling option premium provides the best chance for success. When searching for which option strategy is the most profitable, too many traders get sucked into get-rich-quick schemes. By falling under the spell of fake gurus and scams, you will only end up losing money.
The truth is, day traders do not earn a profit and popular options trading gurus are lying to their followers. David Jaffee shares the trades that he sends to his trade alerts subscribers on YouTube. David Jaffee believes that it's possible to win ~95%+ of your trades by selling option premium. There is no way to make a million dollars overnight right out of the gate, unless you win the lottery.
The best way to make a profit trading options is by selling option premium. It may not be the most complex option strategy or fast-paced, but it is consistent and reliable. You do NOT want the most complex option strategy, instead you should strive for a simple strategy that has a high probability of profit which you can easily implement. If you want to make a living trading options, selling option premium is the only way to go.

Can you use an options calculator?

Some traders, especially those who are new to the game or inexperienced, see profit calculators as a shortcut. Unfortunately, you cannot cheat your way to success. Using an options calculator may provide some quick results, but they are not sustainable. You need knowledge and experience to really be successful trading options. If you rely on an options calculator without investing your time in learning the ropes, you are throwing your money away.

Learn the Best Option Strategy Ever

You can waste a lot of time searching for the most profitable options strategy reddit feed or watching YouTube videos that promise instant success. Or, you can invest your time wisely and learn from a successful options trader because many people consider David Jaffee to be the best options trading coach. While there is no options strategies cheat sheet, you can learn the best options trading strategy to maximize your returns while reducing risk.
David Jaffee offers a comprehensive online options trading course providing a complete breakdown of the most profitable options trading strategy.

Safe Option Strategies To Boost Your Trading Profits

I have written about incorporating options as part of your investing arsenal on several occasions. Options are often seen as a leverage tool, often viewed through the lens of fear and bewilderment. However, the truth is that options as an investing tool are not DANGEROUS. People ARE.
Options at the end of the day are just a financial product that provides you immense flexibility to structure your trades based on a myriad of factors such as your bullish/bearish view, time horizon, confidence level, etc.
It is often GREED in humans that makes options trading "risky".
As mentioned, the primary idea behind options lies in the strategic use of leverage. If done systematically, options trading can be safer than purchasing stocks directly. Why so?

Let's take for example one is bullish on a stock such as Fastly which is currently trading at US$102/share. Purchasing 100 shares of Fastly will entail a capital commitment of US$10,200. One can get the same 100 shares exposure to Fastly by purchasing 1 Call Option (equivalent to 100 shares) Assume one spends US$1,000 to purchase an Option with a contract expiration of 65 days. This is the max amount that one can lose in this scenario.

On the other hand, by purchasing physical shares, there is a risk of a significant "gap down" which results in more losses than what you might expect. You might have entered at US$102, placing a 10% "Stop Loss" level. This is the "maximum" amount of risk you are willing to take which equates to US$1,020 in losses. However, if the price gaps down by 20% overnight (Fastly gaps down by 30% after a weak set of management guidance), your max loss is now at US$2,040 vs. your original US$1,020 expectations.
On the other hand, by spending US$1,000 on the call option contract, you know with 100% certainty that this is the maximum amount of loss you will incur. At the end of the day, a good options strategy to deploy takes into consideration the investor's goals as well as the overall market climate.

Is Selling Option a superior strategy vs. Buying Option?

In my opinion, selling options is not always "superior" compared to option buying, as widely advertised by options trainer who claims that 90% of options trade expire worthless, so it does not make sense to purchase/buy options as you have only got a 10% probability rate of making some money out of it.
I believe that options buying and selling are both relevant options strategies. You just need to know your investment goal and the context in which you are executing these option strategies. Are you going directional? Do you have a lower risk appetite? Etc. With that in mind, let's take a look at some of the safest options strategies out there in the market.

Safe Option Strategies #1: Covered Call

Safe option strategies (covered Call)
The covered call strategy is one of the safest option strategies that you can execute. In theory, this strategy requires an investor to purchase actual shares of a company (at least 100 shares) while concurrently selling a call option. Take for example I am bullish on Philip Morris (PM) shares and I own 100 shares of the counter for US$70/share. My total outlay is US$7,000 on this counter.
I can look to reduce my total capital outlay on the counter by SELLING one call option on PM, thus generating an income to offset my total cost. Say, for example, I sell a 4-months call option on PM (expiring in 128 days), generating a premium of US$0.40/share or US$40/contract at a strike price of US$90/share.

On expiration, if the share price of PM remains at or below US$90/share, the call options expire worthless and I get to keep my full premium amount of US$40. I can look to repeat the same process by selling another call option on PM and continue to generate income from this strategy.

If the share price of PM is above US$90/share on expiration, I no longer am able to participate in any further upside of PM since the 100 shares I originally own will be called (or to put it simply sold) away at US$90/share.

In this scenario, my total gain is $90-$70=$20 plus 0.40 (option premium) = $20.40/share or an ROI of 29% over 4-months equivalent to an annualized ROI of c.87%. Pretty decent I would say.

If you are already comfortable owning 100 shares of a particular counter, the covered call strategy adds ZERO downside risk to your holdings. It will help to reduce your overall investment cost. The key "downside" is that you will not be able to partake in the upside if there is a strong rally in the shares.

What type of shares is suitable for covered call strategies?

In my opinion, such a strategy is quite useful for dividend-paying stocks such as PM. I have written about why the covered call strategy is one of my favorite strategies when it comes to executing a high dividend-yielding stock such as PM in this article: Philip Morris: How to put its 6% yield on steroids.

One, since you own the physical shares of PM, you will be entitled to the dividends paid by the counter. In this case, a juicy 6% yield. This might be the preferred option compared to a Poor Man's Covered Call (PMCC) where an investor structuring a PMCC will not be entitled to the dividends. More on that later.

Two, it is not particularly expensive to own 100 shares of PM since it is not exactly a "high-priced" counter. Hence, I am comfortable with forking out US$7,000 to purchase 100 shares of PM. This might not be possible for a "high-priced" dividend-paying stock such as Broadcom (AVGO) for example, a counter which is priced at US$375/share, thus owning 100 shares will entail a capital commitment of US$37,500 in this example. In general, if you have the intention of holding shares of a company long-term while continue to earn dividend income, a covered call strategy might just be the ideal safe options strategy to turbo-charge your income potential.

You don't need to execute the covered call strategy only on dividend-paying stocks. Some might also say that such a strategy turns a non-dividend-paying stock into one. Professional traders often use covered calls to improve the earnings from their investment.

Selling call options are also particularly "ideal" when volatility is high. Hence, an investor might wish to sell a call option on his long-term shareholdings when volatility is elevated. Ideally, this is done with a short date-to-expiration (DTE) since time value decay is the fastest in the last 2-3 months of an option contract horizon.

Key Risks

Not able to partake in further upside appreciation of the stock more than the Sell Call Strike

Unlike stocks where you can control the number of shares you wish to purchase (ie, you can just go for 1 share if you like), purchasing/selling 1 Option Contract is equivalent to having exposure of 100 shares. To make the covered call strategy safe, you will need to own AT LEAST 100 shares of the underlying stock. This might be a significant commitment and you will still be substantially exposed to a substantial fall in the underlying share price.

Safe Option Strategies #2: Buying Diagonal Spreads

Safe option strategies (buy diagonal spreads)
A diagonal spread strategy involves the investor to get into a long and short option position on the same asset but with different expirations and different strike prices
So, for example, I PURCHASE a long-DTE call option on a stock such as FB while simultaneously SELLING a short-DTE call option on the same stock FB. Using some numbers as context, FB is currently trading at US$275/share. I purchase an ATM option of FB with a strike of US$270 and expiring in 310 days-time, paying a premium of $4,160 ($500 in Intrinsic value and $3,660 in time value). Concurrently, I sell a call option with a strike of US$300 expiring in 37 days-time, generating a premium of US$400. My total outlay for this calendar spread is $4,160 – $400 = $3,760.
The primary idea behind this strategy is that as expiration dates get closer, time decay accelerates. So, in this example, since I SOLD the near-DTE option, I will want its value to get to ZERO ASAP. The accelerating time-value decay for the short-DTE option contract benefits me in this instance.
When the short-DTE option expires (in 37 days-time) and the price of FB remains below US$300/share, the contract becomes worthless and my profit is the full US$400 amount. I will be left with an outstanding long call option with approx. 270 days left to expiration. I can then structure another diagonal spread by selling a short-DTE call option again (another 30 days) and generate another round of premium which will look to further reduce my cost.
The Poor Man's Covered Call (PMCC) which I have written quite extensively in this article, is an example of a diagonal spread. One where you buy a long-DTE Deep In-the-money (ITM) call option and selling a short-DTE Out-of-the-money (OTM) call option.
What type of shares is suitable for buying diagonal spreads?
The PMCC is a cheaper alternative compared to the covered call strategy, the latter requiring the ownership of at least 100 shares in a counter.

For "high-priced" stocks, that might be costly. Instead, buying a Deep ITM call option achieves a similar effect of owning physical shares of the stock but yet at a much cheaper cost. For example, to purchase 100 shares of FB, that might entail an outlay of US$27,500 in today's context.

Structuring a PMCC might mean paying $8,400 (436 days DTE with 0.80 Delta) for the long leg of the option which is less than 30% of the capital requirement vs. actual stock ownership. This capital outlay can be further reduced by selling a short-DTE (37 days) call option with a strike of $300, generating a premium of $400. Net Outlay = $8,400 – $400 = $8,000 vs.$27,500 (29% cost capital of physical stock ownership)

Structuring a diagonal spread like the PMCC is useful for "high price" stocks vs. covered call structure. Since a PMCC structure is not entitled to any dividends (holding a long call option does not entitle you to dividends), there is no added incentive of owning the stock outright for a non-dividend-paying counter.

In this sense, a diagonal spread structure might be a cheaper alternative without "forgoing" the dividends in question because there is none to speak of.

Lastly, my personal stock preference for diagonal spreads are selecting stable counters without significant price fluctuation, ideally counters with Beta less than 1.0. This will avoid the situation of pre-maturely selling, something which I will cover in the next segment.

Pre-mature exit – an in-depth example

If one is purchasing a diagonal spread structure as illustrated above (buying long-DTE ITM call options and selling short-DTE OTM call options), the major "additional" risk, similar to the covered call scenario, is that of pre-maturely exiting the trade and thus not able to enjoy the full upside potential in the event the stock witnessed a strong short-term bump in price.

In our FB example, we bought a long-DTE call option at a strike of $270 while simultaneously selling a short-DTE call option at a strike of $300. The key risk is that FB price appreciates significantly, beyond $300/share over the next 1-month. Assume that FB share price closes at $310/share on the short-call expiration, as the seller, we will be obligated to sell at $300/share, thus making a loss of $10/share or $1,000 on this contract. However, this will be more than compensated by the long call option contract which was purchased with a strike of $270, hence there will be at least $40/share in intrinsic value ($310-$270) and since there is still plenty of time left, we assume that the time value dropped from the original $36.60 to $30. So potentially your long call will be worth $40 in intrinsic value and $30 in time value for a total value of $70.

Subtract the $10/share losses and your original net cost of $37.60 and your net profit will be $12.40 or $1,240. Still a decent profit over a short duration but now you will not be able to partake in further upside in the price of FB (unless you roll the short leg, which will be an article for another day).

Key risks associated with buying diagonal spreads

So again, the only "additional" risk associated with purchasing a diagonal spread is that your trade might be pre-maturely "closed", without you be able to partake in further upside.

Similar to the covered call strategy, you will still be making losses if the price of FB drops substantially. However, the maximum loss is capped at the net premium which you pay for the diagonal spread. This is significantly lower compared to owning 100 shares of the underlying shares which might head to ZERO, no matter how unlikely that scenario might be.

In our example, if FB goes to zero (yes, I know it's highly unlikely), the max amount of losses we will incur is $8,000 through the diagonal spread strategy vs. $27,500 if we own 100 shares of the stock.

The additional risk associated with BUYING diagonal spreads is generally "low". The inverse is SELLING diagonal spreads which entail a strategy of selling a long-DTE option at a lower strike and buying a short-DTE option at a higher strike.

So for the FB example, I will be selling the long-DTE ATM $270 strike, thus receiving a premium of $4,160, and buying the short-DTE OTM $300 strike, paying a premium of $400. My net premium received is $3,760. I am essentially "bullish" in the short-term while "bearish" in the long-term. Such a strategy becomes of a much higher risk nature because FB could potentially appreciate substantially, resulting in massive losses on our short leg (long-DTE ATM $270 strike). This is not something that a new option trader should be engaging in.

Safe Option Strategies #3: Buying/Selling Verticals

3 Safe Option Strategies better than stock buying 1
3 Safe Option Strategies better than stock buying 2
A vertical options trade consists of 2 legs, similar to the diagonal spread. You go long an option and short an option with different strikes. However, the expiration period is the same. That is the key difference between a vertical as well as a diagonal spread.

Types of verticals – Debit vs. Credit

A vertical can be a debit strategy (one in which you pay a premium) or a credit strategy (one in which you receive a premium). A call debit spread (or a bull call spread) is one that you pay for the spread. How this is structured is generally purchasing a long call with a strike price that is lower than the strike price of the call you sold. So, again using FB as an example, you can structure a call debit spread by purchasing a call option with a strike at $270 with DTE of 310 days, paying $4,160, and selling a call option with a strike of $300 with the SAME DTE of 310 days, receiving $2,800 in premium.

Your total net outlay will be $4,160 – $2,800 = $1,360 (max risk)

Your max profit = $1,640

Depending on how one structures the vertical, the risk: reward potential will be substantially different. However, again, you have a defined maximum risk. In this example, it is $1,360, substantially lower than purchasing a single leg call option where the premium outlay is $4,160.

What is the difference between buying and selling a vertical?

When we buy a vertical, we pay a premium while selling a vertical will result in us receiving a premium. Both buying and selling will see our RISK as well as PROFIT potential being defined.

If that is the case, why should anyone be wishing to pay for a vertical (debit strategy) instead of selling a vertical (credit strategy) when the latter strategy results in generating cash straight into our pocket? The key reason is because of the difference in risk: reward potential.

When you BUY a vertical, your IDEAL structure will be one where your reward potential is MORE than your risk level in most circumstances. How much more? That will be a topic for another day. When you SELL a vertical, typically you will be selling a short-DTE vertical where both legs are OTM to benefit from the effect of accelerating time value decay. In this case, your risk: reward potential will be substantially lower than 1, ie you risk $1 to make $0.30 for example.

Why will anyone do that? That is because the probability of you making the $0.30 is much higher than the probability of you losing that $1. Again, this is something that proponents of option selling will highlight time and again (much higher probability to WIN even though the profit potential is much lower than the at-risk amount).

Verticals vs. 1 Leg Option

So why is buying/selling verticals a "safer" strategy compared to just executing a 1 leg option? First, when you buy a vertical, you reduce your capital outlay vs. simply buying a call/put option. This is also your max loss. With a lower capital outlay (most of the time roughly 30-40% lower vs. 1 leg option), you thus reduce your break-even level and correspondingly increase your Probability of Profit.

Second, the key risk associated with selling a 1 leg (or naked) option is that your losses can be very substantial. When you structure a vertical, you are essentially like an "insurance company buying reinsurance". That is an analogy that I often use.

For example, when you sell a put option at a strike of $50, you are essentially insuring the buyer of the put option of any downside risk associated with the stock below the price of $50. If the price of the stock collapse to $0, your losses as the insurance company will be massive.

On the other hand, if you purchase reinsurance by using part of the premium that you received from selling the put option at a strike of $50 and now BUY a put option at a lower strike of $45, your losses will be "capped" at $5/share (exclude net premium received) in this example.

Proper structure of a vertical makes it a safe option strategy

Whether you are buying or selling a vertical, your profit and losses are defined. You know right from the start your max potential profit and loss.

Knowing that fact makes the vertical strategy a safe options strategy suitable for a beginner options trader to execute. While I am not overly concerned about the risk associated with buying verticals, a well-defined strategy is needed when it comes to selling verticals. This is because of its lower reward to risk ratio. While one might argue that it has a higher probability of profit vs. buying, a couple of really bad trades could substantially affect your trading account.

Key risks associated with trading verticals

Potential "over-leveraging" because capital outlay is much smaller than buying 1 leg option or purchasing stocks

Significantly higher probability of losing your entire capital outlay

In conclusion, the above 3 options strategies, if done in a proper manner, are potentially safe option strategies that a new option trader can look to execute. The covered call strategy is an ideal method to put your dividend-generating stocks on steroids. However, do note that one will need at least 100 shares of the underlying stock to execute a covered call strategy. Buying diagonal spreads is a cheaper alternative vs. covered call. This can be executed on "high price" stocks, non-dividend or low-dividend paying stocks with beta less than 1.0

Last but not least, verticals are safe option strategies that are not overly complicated, with the trader knowing from the onset his/her max risk and profit potential. When it comes to selling verticals, one should engage a proper trade mechanism to increase your long-term chances of success when it comes to deploying such a strategy to generate a consistent and steady flow of income every month.

Conclusion

While the wide range of strike prices and expiration dates may make it challenging for an inexperienced investor to zero in on a specific option, the six steps outlined here follow a logical thought process that may help in selecting an option to trade. Define your objective, assess the risk/reward, look at volatility, consider events, plan out your strategy, and define your options parameters.

Options are among the most popular vehicles for traders, because their price can move fast, making (or losing) a lot of money quickly. Options strategies can range from quite simple to very complex, with a variety of payoffs and sometimes odd names. (Iron condor, anyone?). While options are normally associated with high risk, traders have a number of basic strategies that have limited risk. And so even risk-averse traders can use options to enhance their overall returns. However, it's always important to understand the downside to any investment so that you know what you could possibly lose and whether it's worth the potential gain.

www.ingramcontent.com/pod-product-compliance
Lightning Source LLC
LaVergne TN
LVHW081526060526
838200LV00044B/2020